Instructio

MW00440823

LET AUGMENTED REALITY CHANGE HOW YOU READ A BOOK

With your smartphone, iPad or tablet you can use the **Hasmark AR** app to invoke the augmented reality experience to literally read outside the book.

1. Download the **Hasmark app** from the **Apple App Store** or **Google Play**

2. Open and select the (vue) option

3. Point your lens at the full image with the and enjoy the augmented reality experience.

Go ahead and try it right now with the Hasmark Publishing International logo.

"Lili's an amazing young woman, who is wise beyond her years. Her story will inspire you in ways that may surprise you. This is an exceptional story that kept me captivated from the first page all the way through to the end. I literally could not put this book down. I highly recommend it to everyone of every age."

—Peggy McColl,
New York Times Best-Selling Author
http://PeggyMcColl.com

"Devastating realities of how abuse and neglect can alter a child's life are simply stated in this true story of one girl's journey. Not just another story, but a heart-felt truth of abuse and neglect told through the eyes of a child.

As a psychotherapist for over 25 years, I have seen how the trauma of abuse and neglect forever changes how one sees the world. Having at least one strong, positive support person in an abused person's life can provide the needed hope for a positively changed future.

Lili's journey is far from over but her hope for being a world changer and helping others understand the effects of abuse and neglect will continue to empower her and readers of her story."

—Denise J. Weaver, L.C.S.W., Ph.D.,
Crossville Counseling Center, P.C.

"This book went right into my heart. It made me emotional, but it also made me hopeful. This book presents an opportunity! Just think about how it can help many young people like Lili. This is Lili's story, but it might also be yours. You are not alone, so please read it, young or old, don't miss out.

I recommend it warmly."

—Ki is your host,
author of Walk Tall:
Create your Own Self-Confidence

"My heart is bleeding. All I can say is that this is one of the best books I have ever read. This story will stay with me my entire life. How Lili and Deb managed to face all their terrible situations with such confidence and joy is hard to visualize! The way the author has written this story brings it straight to your heart and you will feel it deeply.

This book is filled with tremendous changes, emotions, motivation, inspiration, and most importantly, love. I highly recommend you read this book no matter what your age is or what is going on in your life. I can promise that if you read at least the first two short chapters, you will be drawn to read the rest of it for sure. Enjoy the read!"

—Sam Mishra

Lili's story displays courage, resilience and bravery. She used the disruptions and confusion in her life to propel her forward even if she was weeping. This compelling book will remind you that you don't have to live with a victim mindset but a victorious mindset. God's love kept Lili safe through every interruption in her life.

Roslyn Rice
Bestselling Author of Power Of One:
Finding Hope In The Midst Of Struggle

OVERCOMING
my mother's
ADDICTIONS

Written by:

Deb Birdsall

In collaboration with Lili Birdsall

Hasmark
PUBLISHING
INTERNATIONAL

Editor: Harshita Sharma | harshita@hasmarkpublishing.com
Cover Design: Anne Karklins | anne@hasmarkpublishing.com
Book Design: Amit Dey | amit@hasmarkpublishing.com
Illustrations: Ereny Emil | Facebook.com/erooemil

ISBN 13: 978-1-77482-036-0
ISBN 10: 1774820366

Dedication

*This book is dedicated to my loving husband, Phil,
who had absolutely no idea what he was getting
into when he married me.
And yet, he continues to stay.*

*I would not have wanted to walk this path without
your unconditional love and support. You are an amazing
man and a wonderful grandfather!*

Contents

Preface

We live in a world where so many of our children face the challenges of dealing with an addicted parent. The choices of the parent have a ripple effect, causing long-lasting consequences for so many family members. Children who have grown up in such an environment have tragically experienced horrific situations in their homes—including neglect, abuse, and domestic violence. As a result, many grandparents find themselves in the position of taking in and raising their grandchildren; trying to balance their retirement years with the need to protect, nurture, and raise small children.

This book is a true story written from the perspective of a now 11-year-old child who has experienced incredibly challenging times. Here, she shares her perspective and the belief systems that have kept her whole and positive. This work depicts actual events in our lives, as truthfully as recollection permits, of experiences over time and/or that can be verified by research. Occasionally, dialogue consistent with the character or nature of the person speaking has been supplemented or recreated. Some events have been compressed. All persons within are actual individuals; there are no composite characters. The names of all individuals have been changed to respect their privacy, except for my granddaughter Lili.

The views and opinions expressed in the book are mine and do not necessarily reflect or represent the views and opinions held by individuals whose characters are portrayed in the book.

I have chosen to write the book from the voice of my granddaughter. Although I cannot know all her thoughts and feelings, she has collaborated with me as the writing of the book has progressed.

I would like to thank the real-life members of the families portrayed in this book for taking my granddaughter into their homes and accepting her as one of their own. I recognize that their memories of the events described in this book may be different than that of my own.

The intent in writing this story is to create an avenue for many people to develop a better understanding of the impact that addiction in the family has on a child.

My hope is it will help many pre-teens and teens to understand that they are not alone in their experiences. I want them to know that the choices their parents may have made do not have to negatively impact their present and future lives. It is also meant to inspire grandparents to cherish their new responsibilities and to relax into their role by recognizing the incredible value their sacrifices bring to their grandchild's life.

I strongly believe that through this book, communication will be opened between teachers, counselors, and children to provide an avenue to discuss this complicated topic in order to get children the appropriate help that they need.

And, finally, it is my deepest wish that many addicts will take this message to heart and be inspired to move into a place of recovery. By making good choices, not only will they benefit, but their children will be blessed as well.

Deb Birdsall – Lili's blessed Grandma

Chapter 1

A few days before I turned 11, my grandma told me something surprising. She said the moment I was born was an incredibly special moment. She was right there when I was pulled from my mother's belly, and she immediately "heard" these words in her head: "This child will be a peace-maker ... the next Henry Kissinger of the world!" Just what is a ten-year-old supposed to do with that kind of information?!?

Before I get into all that, let me tell you a little about myself. My name is Liliana Renee. My family and friends call me Lili. I am black and I am white. My half sisters are Hispanic. I am kind, spiritual, loving, and fun. I am a good listener and love to laugh. I am a school cheerleader. I can do splits and backbends and love to do gymnastics! My friends trust me because they know that I will always be there for them, in good times and bad.

I was born during a major snowstorm. Cold, white snow was falling in huge flakes with the wind whipping it around so hard that you couldn't even see the road. As it turns out, that was an appropriate beginning to the childhood I was soon to experience.

You see, in the first ten years of my life, I lived with four different families a total of eight different times! I'm going to share with you what has happened in my life so far, as I recall it, and I don't want to scare you because it all has a happy ending. Because of all that I have gone through, I have learned some incredibly valuable lessons already in my life. Maybe they can help you, too.

Chapter 2

My grandma has always called me an old soul, but my mom is what you would probably call a lost soul. When she was my age, 11, she decided to start using drugs. Her choices from that day forward created the path that eventually made me who I am today.

My grandma shared with me that when my mom was 18 years old, she got caught stealing two CDs from a store. She chose to argue with the police officer. To make a point, he decided to let her sit in jail overnight. It was the same night that my mom met the man who later became my biological father.

I first learned from my grandma that Mom used drugs the whole time she was pregnant with me. Things got so bad that her friends didn't want to throw her a baby shower because they weren't sure I would even be born alive.

My grandma stepped in and convinced my mom to go to a doctor who prescribed medication that kept her high, but not so much that it would keep hurting me. The doctor was afraid that if she stopped using the drugs while she was pregnant, I might not live!

Two days before I was born, my biological father flew in from another state to be there for my birth. The day after I was born, he refused to sign the papers that would list him as my father. He left the hospital, got on a plane, and simply left my life. I've never met him. I didn't even know his name until recently.

Not feeling wanted can really mess with your head. Fortunately, I understand that his decision to not have me in his life is not about me. I really believe that my life is better off without him in it and feel that he is the one who has missed out by not signing the papers.

Chapter 3

When I was three months old, my mom moved to be near my grandma and grandpa. They were living in a motorhome in an RV resort.

While Mom worked as a waitress, I got to spend my time playing at the resort on the playground, learning to swim in the pool, and riding around in the back of a golf cart with Grandma and Grandpa. It was great visiting with them almost every day. When I was about a year old, my grandma tried to call my mom one afternoon and couldn't get an answer. Grandma came to our trailer and found my mom passed out from drugs. I guess I hadn't been fed or changed in a while.

Mom said that she wasn't using any drugs and offered to take a drug test to prove that she was able to keep me with her and take care of me. But when Grandma gave her the drug test to do, Mom poured bleach in the cup, knowing it would mess up the results.

Grandma got my mom into a drug rehab, but she only stayed a couple of weeks before she got kicked out for sneaking out and using drugs. When they brought Mom back home, Grandma tried to reason with her as to why she needed to get help, but instead she just threatened to kill herself.

I guess that you can't help someone if they don't want the help. Grandma learned at an Al-Anon meeting that you can't make a person drink or use drugs if they don't want to, and you can't keep them from drinking or using drugs if that is what they really want to do. In other words, no matter how much we want to help, we don't have any control over other people's actions. That's a tough lesson to learn.

Chapter 4

When I was almost three, my mom married a man named Carlos. He was a hardworking man who loved my mom and me very much. Carlos and Mom were together off and on since I was five months old. He tried to help her with her addiction, but he would get frustrated and would be in and out of our lives.

The day they got married, I was the flower girl. I walked down the aisle in my pretty red dress, dropping rose petals along the way. My mom looked beautiful in her white wedding dress and Carlos was so handsome in his tuxedo. A lot of people were there to celebrate and Carlos' parents in Central America even got to watch the wedding on their computer.

Mom and my new daddy bought a nice mobile home and I had my own bedroom with lots of pretty furniture. Mom even painted the walls my favorite color: pink! I thought everything was going to be good from then on. Boy, was I wrong!

Within a month or so after we moved into our new home, Mom and Dad started fighting a lot. Dad would come home very tired after working all day and he would find Mom, high on drugs, laying around the house. The house would be a terrible mess and Dad would get very mad. He and Mom would yell back and forth at each other. Even though they would send me to my room, I could still hear it all happening and I couldn't do anything about it. And yes, I was scared.

It was at that time when Rosie came to me. My mom called her my imaginary friend, but Rosie wasn't imaginary to me at all. She would sit next to me and tell me that everything was going to be okay. She told me that Jesus was watching over me and holding me in his arms. She taught me how to pray to God for peace. When Rosie was with me, I felt very safe.

My grandma told me later that Rosie was my guardian angel. I am so thankful she was there for me when things were so awful.

Chapter 5

One afternoon, things got so bad that my mom called my grandma. Mom was screaming into the phone that Daddy was trying to kill her. She kept saying that she was going to leave for good. I didn't know if she was going to take me with her or not.

Grandma came to our house and saw Mommy and Daddy screaming and hitting each other. All this while Mom was holding onto me really tight.

Grandma tried to get Mom to calm down and she finally did a little bit. Mom said that she had to go to work, so Grandma dropped her off and took me home with her. During her shift, Mom borrowed a friend's car, bought drugs, and took them. Then, because of being high, she ran the car into a guardrail and drove back to work. She was waiting on customers and not talking clearly, so her boss came in and fired her from her job.

The next morning Grandma and Grandpa went to the judge and got emergency custody of me. Mom had to go to the court. She told the judge that Grandma and

Grandpa could keep me for a couple of weeks while she "got her life together".

Grandma talked to Mom and told her that if she went to a drug rehab program and got help, they would take care of me while she was there. Then, once she graduated from the program, I could go back to live with her. Grandma also told Mom that if she didn't stay the whole eight to ten months and graduate from the program, she would find a family to adopt me. Grandma said that I deserved to be with a loving family and in a safe environment.

Mom only stayed in the program four and a half months. During that time, she threatened to leave four different times. Finally, she checked herself out and within two days, she was back to using drugs again. Now, you need to understand that Grandma has never been one to make threats. Once she comes to a decision, she always follows through.

Chapter 6

After leaving rehab, Mom left the state we were all living in. She moved from house to house and friend to friend, until each of them would get tired of her stealing their money and lying to them.

After ten months of me living with my grandparents, my grandma decided it would be best for me to have a loving family adopt me so that I could live a full and joyful life. She and Grandpa worked together to find a family that would give me every opportunity for love and success and who would still let them be a part of my life.

I was three years old when, through an adoption agency, Grandma and Grandpa finally decided on a couple. I called them Mommy Karen and Daddy Kevin. They were wonderful people. They took me to church a couple times a week. I met lots of different kinds of people—rich, poor, black, Hispanic, white, old, and young. I learned more about Jesus and how much He loves me. Over the next fourteen months, as Mommy Karen and Daddy Kevin worked through the process of adopting me, their family became my family. Their parents became my grandparents and I got lots of new aunts and uncles and cousins as well.

I got to go to a private Christian pre-school and made many friends there while learning more about how God works in my life. Things were going great, and once again in my life, I felt safe and happy.

My grandma always told me that we can never have too many parents, grandparents, brothers, and sisters, and that they don't have to be blood-related to be our family. She also let me know how lucky I was to have so very many people who loved me and saw me for the special person that I am.

Chapter 7

By the time I was almost four years old, everyone was working hard so that I could be adopted by Mommy Karen and Daddy Kevin. Then my mom decided that she wanted me back. She got a lawyer who asked the judge to give me back to my mom.

Grandma and the adoption attorney tried to convince the judge that it would not be good for me to go back to living with my mom. An attorney, who the court said was "my attorney," told the judge that she had met with everyone and that she felt that it would be dangerous to return me to my mother. The judge took a break and while Daddy Kevin was standing in the hallway, he overheard a man tell my mom that she didn't need to worry. He said that some people had already talked to the judge and "everything had been taken care of."

So, even though my mom was going to have another baby soon and was still using drugs, the judge decided to take me away from Mommy Karen and Daddy Kevin and put me back with her. It all happened so fast.

The judge said I had one week before I had to go back to living with my mom. When the week was up, Grandma and Grandpa came to pick me up and take me to my mom. Everyone was crying. I was so confused and upset. I was four years old and really sad.

Chapter 8

My stepdad, Carlos, bought a restaurant and worked from early in the morning to late at night, so I didn't get to see him very much.

Shortly after my half sister Leah was born, Mom got pregnant again. When Alexis was born, she had drugs in her body. Child Protective Services told Mom that she wasn't allowed to be alone with us at home, so she slept in the storage shed at the restaurant.

Daddy would go to work, and we had someone else taking care of us at home. After a while, Mom lied to Daddy and told him that the judge said she could come back home, and she did.

Most days, Mom wouldn't get out of bed until the afternoon. So, when I was only five years old, I would get up and make bottles for my baby sisters, feed them, change them, and rock them to keep them quiet. Unless we went to the restaurant at night, sometimes I would only get one microwave bowl of macaroni and cheese to eat each day. I was really happy on the days I could eat two bowls.

Mom was supposed to take me to school in the mornings, but most of the time she didn't get up on time and I would get to school late. The people at the school didn't like that. They called Mom and Daddy and told them that they would be in trouble if they didn't get me to school every day and on time.

One day when I woke my mom up to take me to school, she put us girls in the car and then went back into the house. When she didn't come out for a long time, I went in and found her lying on the floor with a needle in her arm. I woke her up and she drove me to school. On the way back home, she drove over the center line in the road and hit another car. Then, she left the accident scene and took my baby sisters to somebody's house and told them to call my dad. When the police came, they found out that my sisters had been in the car during the accident, so they arrested my mom for child endangerment. That meant that she had to spend five months in jail.

When she got out of jail, she kept stealing money from Daddy's business so she could buy drugs. He would buy a TV for us and she would sell it to get more drugs. I remember seeing Daddy starting to drink more alcohol and when he got drunk, he could get mean. He and Mom would end up screaming and swearing at each other. I would see them hit each other and break things in the house.

Mom and Daddy would yell at each other, and I would have to hide in my bedroom. I would scream at them to stop and then sometimes they would get mad at me and hit me. At times, the police would come to the door. It was all very scary for me.

But even during those hard times, there were good things that happened. My grandma helped Mommy Karen and Daddy Kevin find two other children to adopt. Heather was ten and Braxton was nine. My mom finally decided to let me spend some weekends and holidays with them, so we all got to be a family. It was great—until I would have to go back home to my mom's house.

Chapter 9

These terrible things went on until finally, when I was seven and a half years old, my grandma had to step in again to help my sisters and me. Daddy and Mom had another fight, and this time, Daddy hit my mom really hard and left bruises on her. Grandma talked Mom into calling the police to report it and then my daddy was arrested. That's when we found out that my mom wasn't supposed to be alone in the house with us after all.

After Daddy got out of jail, the police told him that he couldn't be around my mom. The very next day, he got caught riding in the car with her. He was arrested again and ended up getting sent back to Central America, which is where he had grown up.

I didn't know it, but I guess he was living in our country illegally. Grandma and Grandpa took all three of us girls to live in their house. Leah was three and Alexis was only two years old at that time.

After Daddy had to return to his country, Mom tried to run the restaurant for a while. But she kept taking the money and spending it on drugs. Customers who had been into the restaurant kept telling my grandma that they were worried about my mom because of how she was acting. At the time, Mom was on something called "probation," which meant that the courts told her that if she used any drugs illegally, she would go back to jail.

One day, Grandma got a call that my mom was passed out in a chair behind the restaurant. The police were called and they took her back to jail for another eight months.

I remember Grandma taking my sisters and me to visit Mom in jail. We would have to talk to her through a big window. It was hard to hear because at the same time, other people would be visiting their families too and everyone would be talking in the same room. Mom would ask me about how school was going. Grandma would hold us up so that we could put our hands on the glass and Mom would do the same so that we could almost touch each other.

Grandma tried to convince Mom to go back into rehab once she got out, but Mom just kept saying that "rehabs don't work" and that she wasn't going back to rehab. Grandma told her that in order for rehab to work, she needed to be willing to work the program. She told Mom that her life would be so much better if she would get the help she needed to understand why she used drugs. So far, Mom still hasn't done that.

My mom was a hard worker when she wasn't using a lot of drugs, but the temptation was always more than she could handle. For some reason, drugs were more important to her than her family or anything else. That's what I believe and the way I feel.

I know that Mom truly does love my sisters and me. I know that her life is terrible because of the choices she made, and I can't do anything to help her. I know that she will always be my mom. At the same time, I also know that I cannot be around her because of how it makes my mind and heart feel. I can't trust that she won't hurt me again.

Chapter 10

While Mom was in jail for eight months, my grandma asked me this question: "If you could choose who you would want to live with, who would that be?" I immediately said, "With Mommy Karen and Daddy Kevin!" Grandma told this to my mom. I know it must have been awfully hard for Mom to make the decision, but she finally chose to sign the papers to let me be adopted. So, the day before I started third grade, the judge said I could go to live with Mommy Karen and Daddy Kevin. They had moved, with Heather and Braxton, to another state and were living in a really big house. Each of us had our own room and we had two big dogs and a little one. I felt like I was back where I really belonged. Heather was an awesome big sister and Braxton and I were like any normal brother and sister—fighting and laughing and teasing each other all the time. I started going to a new school and had a wonderful teacher who told me that I was amazing. She said I had gone through more in my young life than she had in all her "years on earth."

We went to church every week. We went to movies and swam in the pool in the backyard all summer long. Mommy Karen and Daddy Kevin were working on the paperwork so that I could finally be adopted.

Grandma and Grandpa would bring my sisters down to see me often and we would have fun together. Sometimes Leah and Alexis would spend the weekend with us so that Grandma and Grandpa could have a little break. Grandma had three surgeries in eight months' time, so Mommy Karen and Daddy Kevin kept Leah and Alexis for a week after Grandma's back surgery.

By this time in my life, I had lived with my mom, then with my grandparents, and after that with Mommy Karen and Daddy Kevin. Then, I went back with my mom and stepdad, back with my grandparents, and again with Mommy Karen and Daddy Kevin—and I was not even eight years old yet!

I felt good. I felt safe. I was happy. Finally, everything seemed wonderful—but only for a little while.

Chapter 11

Shortly before it was time for me to be adopted, some bad things started to happen. I saw that both Mommy Karen and Daddy Kevin were being very mean to Heather. They would use a belt on her if she talked back to them. Heather told me that when she asked them why they used a belt on her but not on me when I got in trouble, they said that once I was adopted, they would start using a belt on me too.

They expected all of us to just say, "Yes, Ma'am" and "No, Sir" to whatever they asked of us and to not question them. Heather was now fourteen years old. Because of the way they treated her, I wonder if Mommy Karen and Daddy Kevin just may not have known how to handle a teenager.

One Sunday, on our way home from church, Daddy Kevin got really mad at Heather about something. When we got out of the car, Daddy told Braxton and me to go into the house.

We went upstairs to a bedroom and watched what was happening outside through the window. We saw them begin to fight and, even though Daddy Kevin and Heather ended up too close to the house for me to see everything going on, Braxton and I could hear a lot of screaming. Heather later told me that Daddy Kevin grabbed her, and they both fell to the ground. She said that he was sitting on top of her, choking her.

When a neighbor came over to see what was happening, Heather got up and ran to another neighbor's house.

The police came to our house and told Daddy Kevin that he wasn't allowed to stay in the house with us until the people from Child Protective Services said he could.

That was five days before I was supposed to be adopted— five days before Heather and Braxton would have legally become my sister and brother.

Mommy Karen called Grandma and said that the adoption was on hold until things were straightened out. That scared Grandma, so she called the people at Child Protective Services and told them that she wanted them to call her if they decided to take us away from Mommy Karen and Daddy Kevin, so she could come get me.

Then she and Grandpa came down for the weekend and kept us kids at a hotel with a swimming pool and talked with each of us about what was going on. Heather told Grandma all the bad things that had been happening and Braxton also told her the same things. I even said to her that I didn't feel safe living in their home anymore. Grandma hugged us and made us promise that when we were interviewed by Protective Services, we would tell them the truth of what we heard, saw and experienced.

A few days later, Protective Services talked to each of us and decided it wasn't safe for us to live with either Mommy Karen or Daddy Kevin. Daddy Kevin was later arrested. They took us kids away and put us in foster homes until the judge could talk to everyone and decide where we would live.

Chapter 12

Heather, Braxton, and I went to live in different foster homes. After a couple of days, they got to live with the same foster family, and I was placed with a foster mom named Sarah. Although it was hard not knowing what was going to happen or how long I would be in foster care, I got really lucky. Sarah was a brand-new foster mom, and she was wonderful. She had only signed up to be an "emergency placement" foster home, which meant that she would only have a kid for a couple of days while Protective Services were trying to find a permanent place for them. I was only the second child that had been placed with her. Sarah was sweet and kind. She really worked hard to make me feel safe.

A few days later, Grandma and Grandpa went to the court to try to get custody of me so I could move back home with them. But because they lived in a different state, the judge told them that they would first have to get approved as foster parents. The attorney hired by Grandma and Grandpa told them that since my mom signed the papers for me to be adopted, by law, they were no longer my grandparents. Grandma told me that she didn't care what the law said; she would always be my grandma. Sarah told Protective Services that she was willing to keep me in her home until Grandma and Grandpa could get custody. They let her do that, which took another eight months!

Sarah's house was in an awesome neighborhood. I made lots of new friends. All the neighbors got together, had block parties, and celebrated birthdays and holidays together.

Grandma and Grandpa came down regularly to visit and Sarah let them stay with us. Sarah worked full-time and had to travel sometimes. That meant that I had to go and stay with other foster parents for a day or two. The other foster families were fun to spend time with.

Sarah worked hard to help me with schoolwork, but I wasn't a great student that year. I think I had too much going on in my mind that kept me from focusing on school. Plus, I really didn't think that I would be staying in the new school for very long.

Sarah made sure that I still got to spend time with Heather and Braxton, and our two foster families did a lot of things together.

Chapter 13

While I was going through all that, Grandma and Grandpa took lots of foster parent classes. They had home inspections and interviews done so that they could be approved to be a foster family.

Just after I turned ten, I was able to go back and live with them. Then we had to wait another six months to go before the judge so that they could get custody of me, and I would no longer be a foster child.

Finally, after a long, long time and a lot of different families, I was adopted by my grandparents and was back in the same school that I had gone to since pre-kindergarten.

Chapter 14

While Grandma and Grandpa were taking foster parent classes, they were also trying to decide what would be best for my sisters, who were still living with them. Grandma made sure that Leah and Alexis talked with Daddy in Central America several times a week. Daddy told Grandma that going back to his country was the best thing that could have happened to him. He said that he knew he made terrible choices and now that he was back with his family, he was involved with his church and doing much better.

Grandma decided to take my sisters to visit Daddy and his family, and found out that they lived in a very safe area and were a wonderful, loving family. After Mom went back to jail the second time, Daddy told Grandma that Mom had been given lots and lots of opportunities to get his girls back and that he would like just one chance to have his daughters live with him again. Grandma decided that Daddy deserved that chance, so she asked the judge to let the girls go live with Daddy. The judge said yes. Grandma said that it was the hardest decision she ever had to make in her life, but she knew that it was the best choice for Leah and Alexis.

Grandma flew my sisters to Central America to live with Daddy and his family. The girls were so happy to be back with their dad. They quickly learned how to speak Spanish. We are planning on visiting them as soon as I get my passport. I can hardly wait!

Chapter 15

I am in fifth grade now. This was a good year at school. I'm making the honor roll. I tried out for the Junior Varsity and Varsity cheerleading squads and got accepted. I love to cheer and am good at remembering the words and movements. Best of all, I have a loud voice so everyone in the stands can hear me.

I decided that I wanted to take part in the Winter Queen pageant. I'd never been in a pageant before. Grandma found me a pretty, full-length lavender-colored dress at a consignment shop. Even though I was very nervous, I walked proudly in front of the judges and was chosen as First Runner-Up out of 40 girls! That was fun. The best part was that one of my best friends won the title. I was so happy for her!

Chapter 16

My grandma understands how important it is for me to have other people to share and talk to about my problems and worries. She takes me to see a wonderful counselor every two weeks so I can talk about what has happened and what is currently going on in my life.

Grandma signed me up for a special program last summer that let me work with horses. In that program, I got to groom the horses. I learned how to ride and control a horse, and myself. I also learned about personal space, believing in myself, and how important it is to have dreams and set goals for my future. I just finished taking leadership training for the program, and this year I will be able to help other kids learn what I have learned.

My lifelong dream, since I was two years old, was to be able to take gymnastics classes. With so much moving around, it had never happened. Then a few months ago, Grandma took me to a gymnastics place and signed me up.

When I went to the first class, they asked me to show them what I could do. I showed them how I had taught myself to do splits, cartwheels, backbends, and things like that. They were so impressed that they immediately moved me from the beginner's class to the intermediate class. I don't think the coach believed me at first when I told her I had taught myself everything. She said, "If you really taught yourself how to do all of this, then you need to do this as a profession!" I love gymnastics and am so happy that I am finally able to fulfill this dream.

Chapter 17

Before I was adopted by Grandma and Grandpa, I asked them to help me make sense of something. I said, "Once you adopt me, then what does that make me to you?" They pointed out that I would legally become their daughter. We decided to have some fun and figured out that my mom then would become my sister and my uncle would be my brother. My little sisters would become my nieces and my great-grandparents would become my grandparents. But Grandma said that no matter what changed, the one thing that would not change is how much she and Grandpa love me and how special I am to them and to God.

When Grandma and Grandpa said they wanted to adopt me, I said that I wanted that, too. But I also told them that they would not be my final adoptive family. My plan is to eventually be adopted by a younger family with children. I have always seen myself growing up with a younger family. One of my grandma's friends and her family have given me a promise ring and have told me that they want to eventually adopt me. They have a son my age! I spend a lot of time with their family now and look forward to when I can be adopted by them.

Chapter 18

My biological father is black, and my mom is white. My grandma says I have the most beautiful skin in the whole wide world. And she's right. I call myself a burnt chicken nugget. I love chicken nuggets!

It has been interesting to see how people who don't know me judge me by the color of my skin. I never dreamed that people would look at me or treat me differently just because I am a mixed-race child. I was wrong!

Grandma told me that when I was a little baby, my mom took me with her into a gas station. When the clerk saw me, she said that I was a "doll baby." She told my mom to enter me into the cutest baby contest at the county fair. There was a man standing behind my mom and he shook his head and said, "Don't bother. There ain't no one down here that's gonna vote for a baby with that skin color!"

Then, when I was in second grade, I was walking down the hall at school. A sixth-grade girl came up to me and said, "Your skin color is different than everyone else. You don't belong here!" When I got home, I told this to my grandma.

She asked me what I said back to the girl. I told her that I was so surprised I couldn't think of anything to say. That's when she said, "The next time that happens—and it will happen again—you smile really big and tell them that your grandma thinks you have the most beautiful skin in the whole wide world!"

Again, when I was in fourth grade, I was sitting with some friends who had darker skin. A boy came up to us and called us "niggers." I got so mad. I stood up, yelled at him and told him he should go home and kill himself. I got into trouble for saying that to him.

When my grandma asked me about it and I told her what happened, she asked me if I thought that, when the boy was born, he came into the world believing that people with different color skin were bad. I told her no. She said, "Unfortunately, kids are taught those beliefs by their families and that hatred causes more hatred." She asked me how I would have felt if that boy had gone home and really killed himself. How would his family have felt if they lost their son?

Grandma then said that when people act in ways toward us that bring hurt, we have two choices—we can react, or we can respond. She explained that reacting is when we talk before we think and then we say hurtful things back. Responding is when we think from our heart and try to help others to better understand why their thinking is not good. She told me that, in the future, when someone says something mean, I can either ignore them or I can tell them I don't appreciate their words and walk away.

Chapter 19

Remember when I said that the moment I was born, my grandma had been "spirit-told" that I would be a peacemaker in the world? One day, Grandma, Grandpa, and I were driving through our little downtown and we noticed people on the courthouse lawn getting ready to do a march against racism.

When I saw that, I told Grandma and Grandpa I had decided that the way I would be a peacemaker is to bring people of all different colors together to understand each other, celebrate how much we are alike, and to appreciate how special and precious our differences are.

Grandma said that she could see me someday standing in front of 50, 5,000, or 500,000 people, saying, "My name is Lili. I didn't get to choose what color my skin was when I was born. If you decide to take time to get to know me and then decide whether to like me or not, that's fine. But, if you decide not to like me because of my skin color, then shame on you, because you and I are 99.5% genetically identical and we are all children of God!"

I can see myself doing that!

Someday I will go to college, get a good job, choose a wonderful husband, and have my own amazing children. Or I might choose to adopt since there are so many kids out there who need good families. Then I will teach them the things that were taught to me and will help them to feel blessed and enjoy happy lives.

Yes, I know what I want in life, and I have always been able to make things happen.

Chapter 20

Grandma and I came up with a list of some of the most important things I have learned so far in my life. She calls them *Lili's Life Lessons*.

I now understand that I have no control over what other people say or do. I know that the things they do and the words they say have nothing to do with me. People act the way they do because of what has happened in their lives. I work hard to make sure I don't let anyone make me feel bad about myself. I also try to see what makes someone act the way they do. When I can put myself in their shoes, it lets me forgive them when they hurt me. My mind and heart are at peace when I can do this.

I also know how important it is to reach out and find at least one person who will love me unconditionally and support me through the tough times. We all need lots of friends. Some should be older than us, and some should be younger. We can learn so much from other people and they can learn from us. I understand it is super important to make sure we let our friends and family know how much we appreciate them. We all just need to know that we are valued and loved.

Gratitude is something that I have learned to practice. In order to feel good and grateful every day, I make a list (sometimes on paper and sometimes in my mind) of all the good things I have in my life. I am blessed to have friends and counselors I feel safe enough to be honest with. This lets me work through any sadness or anger I am feeling. And it also allows me to have people who I can share with when I feel happy. I have learned to trust my feelings and won't let anyone else tell me how I should feel about what is going on in my life.

I know that it is good to help other people as often as we can. There are many people who need help and support. When I help other people, it makes me feel good, too.

Thank goodness I love to move! I exercise. I listen to fun music and dance. I do something every day to keep my energy up and my spirits high. I get to laugh a lot. I love to tease Grandma and Grandpa and they like to tease me back. When we do that, we don't end up taking ourselves too seriously and we have fun.

I understand that it is so important to make good choices about who I spend my time with, and what I watch and read. Those people and ideas will either build me up or cause me to make bad decisions.

And most importantly, I know in my heart that God only makes beautiful people. I also know how much He loves me.

Chapter 21

In fourth grade, I saw a quote from Maya Angelou that said, "Do the best you can until you know better. Then when you know better, do better."

My life isn't perfect, but I choose to make it good. Grandma always told me that when we are faced with problems, we have two choices—we can let it make us a *bitter* person or a *better* person. She said that the difference between the two is whether we decide to complain about it, or we learn from it and use it to help other people. It is my decision to look at the things that have happened as opportunities to make me a nicer and stronger person.

I know that I am not better than anyone else, but I do try to be the best Lili that I can be.

About the Author

Deb Birdsall

Deb lives with her husband Phil and granddaughter Lili in the lovely small town of Crossville, Tennessee, USA.

Deb views her life as a continuous opportunity to learn and grow. She has set two goals for herself everyday: to learn something new and to leave everyone she meets feeling better about themselves.

Deb has spent her life in the pursuit of gaining knowledge and developing wisdom. She has opened herself to finding mentors like Zig Ziglar, Bob Proctor, Peggy McColl, and others to educate her on creating a life that manifests all her heart's desires.

From the age of two, Deb recognized that she had a gift of healing the body, mind, and spirit of others through touch. For the past twenty-six years, Deb has followed her passion as a licensed massage therapist. She incorporates the art and science of working with vibrational energies to open people to their own healing capabilities.

Deb also understands her gift of helping others through the critical transitions in life. She has served as a doula, educating and preparing parents for their pregnancies, labors, and deliveries, and has had the privilege of being involved in the births of thirty babies. At the other end of the spectrum, she has also supported families and held vigil with individuals as they transition out of their physical experience.

As a grandparent raising grandchildren because of drug addiction in the family, Deb Birdsall has set out on a mission to help other grandparents better understand the challenges faced by them and their grandchildren.

She does this by providing strategic assistance to grandparents, showing them how to give their grandchildren the necessary tools to successfully overcome their adverse childhood experiences, thereby creating an opportunity for the children to move into vibrant and emotionally healthy adulthoods.

Deb has a passion for protecting our youth and showing them how to develop self-confidence and a positive outlook on life. Through her programs, she teaches them the steps to develop a strategic plan that will bring them successfully through life.

As a personal development coach, Deb is an expert in inspiring others to gain peace of mind and heart and to create fulfillment of their dreams!

Please visit www.DebBirdsall.com to learn more about available programs and become a part of this critical mission.

Deb Birdsall

Thank you for reading "Overcoming My Mother's Addictions." I hope it touched your heart and inspired you to join us as we bring this very important message to the world.

We realize that this book will open a lot of emotions for many. To continue the process of healing we have created several courses around Lili's Life Lessons for children, grandparents, and foster parents. The programs will inspire and give practical steps to teach the process of Release, Restore and Rebuild which leads to Hope, Health and Happiness.

If you were moved by reading our book, please help us get this message out to the world by providing an Amazon review.

To learn more about how you can help yourself or others to attain this hope, health and happiness, please visit our website.

www.DebBirdsall.com

If you would like to connect personally with Deb, email her at DebBirdsall.Author@gmail.com

A Personal Note from Lili:

The Jonah's Joy PRINCESS program has been very good for me. I have been able to share my story with the other girls who have gone through or are currently experiencing similar situations as me. We learned about the Godly qualities of **Patience, Respect, Integrity, Nobility, Conscientiousness, Ethics, Service and Self-Confidence and how to put those characteristics into practice in our lives.** Please help me support this wonderful organization by making a donation on their website: www.JonahsJoy.org. Thank you!

The mission of Jonah's Joy is to provide a faith-based residential treatment home providing quality mental health services to abused, neglected, and troubled children and their families for the purpose of changing generational cycles of abuse and neglect by educating, training, and holding accountable children and their families.

The residential property will provide a spacious home to house up to twelve girls, with adequate space for group programming, as well as staff and administrative offices. The property will have a barn with 12 stalls for Animal-Assisted Therapy with large horses and small farm animals. The program will include agriculture instruction and development.

Daily activities will consist of a faith-based, positive character-building, structured program that includes going to school, having daily chores, negotiating within a "family system", and learning how to respect authority. The program will be strongly therapeutic in nature, including three hours of individual therapy a week, group therapy daily and family therapy weekly.

Current services include the PRINCESS program and BELOVED 2.0, which are mini-versions of the residential program. These programs are closed small groups that are facilitated by Dr. Weaver and support staff and includes 4 to 6 hours of group therapy weekly over a several month period. The participants are chosen based on similar treatment needs.

Jonah's Joy: Home for Children is a 501c3 (non-profit) organization in Crossville, TN.

To learn more about this important organization and to make a donation, please visit www.JonahsJoy.org.

**THE AUTHOR wishes to thank the
DICK WAGNER REMEMBER THE CHILD
MEMORIAL FUND**,
a 501(c)3 non-profit for allowing us to include Dick
Wagner's song, **"REMEMBER THE CHILD,"**
in our programs to promote healing
and recovery of the spirit.

The Dick Wagner Fund creates and funds music therapy
programs for hospitalized and disabled children.
PLEASE DONATE to SUPPORT!
www.dwrtc.org/donate
Your tax-deductible donation brings the
healing power of music to children.

**Remember the Child
Lyrics and music by Dick Wagner © Desert
Dreams Global Music**, BMI

A B C me crying
Mama make me smile
Rock me in your arms a little while.
A B C me crying
Won't you love your child?

E F G I'm sorry
Daddy, take my hand
Tell me what I've done so bad
E F G I wonder why are you so mad
Don't you love me Dad?

Cross my heart I swear, Ma
I won't cry no more
I'll just lay in silence
Down here on the floor
Cross my heart and hope to die
If you don't want me anymore.

1 2 3 4 you, Ma
I won't talk so loud
I won't laugh so hard
I'll shut my mouth
1 2 3 4 you, Ma
I won't make a sound

Do Re Me and angry words are all I hear
Thru my bedroom walls, Dad, loud and clear
Do Re Me I lie awake and shake with fear
And wish I had no ears

Try to Remember the Child that once was you
Did you hide in the darkest corners
Of your lonely room and pray to God
To help you through the long and lonely nights?
Afraid to holler Mama,
Oh please Come hold me tight

Go on and close your eyes, Mama
Take a little trip through time, Dad
Let it all come back to you
And give unto every child, the love
The love denied to you
And Remember the Child will remember
And Remember the Child will remember
His whole lifetime too....

THE STEP BY STEP GUIDEBOOK OF
SIMPLE CONFIDENCE TOOLS THAT REALLY WORK
Buy it on Amazon - visit www.kiisyourhost.com

Walk
Tall

CREATE YOUR OWN
SELF-CONFIDENCE

BY KI IS YOUR HOST

HEARTS to be HEARD

Giving a Voice to Creativity!

With every donation, a voice will be given to
the creativity that lies within the hearts of
our children living with diverse challenges.

By making this difference, children that may
not have been given the opportunity to have their
Heart Heard will have the freedom to create
beautiful works of art and musical creations.

Donate by visiting

HeartstobeHeard.com

We thank you.

Made in the USA
Middletown, DE
23 December 2021

56794578R10051